BONDAGE

Star Finch

BROADWAY PLAY PUBLISHING INC
New York
www.broadwayplaypublishing.com
info@broadwayplaypublishing.com

BONDAGE
© Copyright 2021 Star Finch

First edition: June 2021
I S B N: 978-0-88145-903-6

Book design: Marie Donovan
Page make-up: Adobe InDesign
Typeface: Palatino

BONDAGE was developed in residency with and originally produced by AlterTheater Ensemble (Producer, Jeanette Harrison) in San Rafael, California, running from 23 March-22 April 2017. Susequently, the play was remounted in San Francisco at A C T's Costume Shop Theater, running from 13-20 January 2018. The cast and creative contributors were:

ZURI .... Dezi Soléy
EMILY .... Emily Serdahl
AZUCAR .... Cathleen Riddley
PHILIP .... Shane Fahy
RUBY .... Emilie Talbot

Director .... Elizabeth Carter
Stage Manager .... Frank Cardinale
Dramaturg .... Duca Knezevic
Costumes .... Natalie Barshow
Co-Space designers .... Jen Brault & Margaret Belton
Sound designer .... Gerry Grosz
Production Manager .... Joel D Eis, M F A

CHARACTERS & SETTING

ZURI, *thirteen. A mulatta house slave.*
AZUCAR, *mulatta house slave.*
PHILIP, *master of the house. Widower. Alcoholic.*
EMILY, *fourteen.* PHILIP'*s only child.*
RUBY, EMILY'*s maternal aunt. Spinster.*

In keeping with the intentions of this play, ZURI *and*
AZUCAR *should always be played by Black actors or those*
who identify as biracial/Black.

This play takes place during Pre-Emancipation on a small
island that has no desire to be witness. The island is an open-
air cage where frogs cry freedom hymns and trees chatter
in disbelief. The surrounding sea is a symphony of salty
suffocation. The island stifles its scream by tunneling bits of
sand-memory into the flesh of its inhabitants, living or dead.

For Avery, Dezi, and Elizabeth

ACT ONE

Scene 1

(In the dark we hear the sound of the ocean. Lights slowly fade up on the dining room. EMILY and ZURI are seated in chairs turned out from the table.)

(Both girls stare off into their own individual daydream for some time. Eventually ZURI begins to move sensually to a rhythm she hums to herself. EMILY studies ZURI in a trance.)

EMILY: Frightening.

ZURI: Pardon?

EMILY: Teach me.
(Beat)
Please.

ZURI: Teach you what?

EMILY: How to move myself the way you do.

ZURI: But there's nothing to teach. I was thinking of something sweet so my body felt sweet too.

EMILY: Then what was the something sweet?

ZURI: Blackberries.

EMILY: You could teach me if you wanted.

ZURI: I promise I couldn't. I don't even recall what I did.

EMILY: Something similar to this.

(She moves in her seat.)

ZURI: I think not.

EMILY: I wish I could go. with you. to pick blackberries.

ZURI: …

EMILY: Will you fasten a scarf around my head, the way you sometimes wear yours?

ZURI: Master Philip said we're not to do that anymore.

EMILY: My father isn't here.

(ZURI reluctantly wraps a long piece of fabric around EMILY's head in an "ethnic" style.)

EMILY: Brush my fine hairs down against my forehead?

ZURI: You have none.

(We hear the sound of footsteps above their heads.)

EMILY: Is anyone upstairs?

(ZURI shakes her head, no.)

(Both girls look up and listen unfazed.)

EMILY: Do you ever wish you were born white, Zuri?

ZURI: What do you mean by "white"?

EMILY: Don't be silly.

ZURI: I'm silly?

EMILY: If I could turn you white I would. I'll grant you that wish should I ever meet a magic fairy in the garden.

ZURI: But my skin is pale now. How much whiter would you wish me?

EMILY: White enough to be free, silly!

ZURI: I would like to be free. But not a "white" free.

EMILY: There is no other kind.

ZURI: A white free would feel like a kind of...death, I'd imagine.

EMILY: Except, I'm not dead.

I wish we were twins, then we'd forget who was who. We'd be one spirit poured into two cups.

ZURI: ...For whom to sip?

(ZURI *has finished tying the scarf. She lowers a silver platter in front of* EMILY'*s face to see her reflection. The platter blocks* EMILY'*s face from the audience's view.*)

EMILY: How lovely!

ZURI: If you're not careful, Emily, people may begin to take you for mulatta.

EMILY: Do you sometimes wish you had hair that spills down your back like mine, Zuri?

(ZURI *places the platter back on the table.*)

ZURI: No.

EMILY: Mmmm, I'd wager you do.
(*Begins to dance in her seat again*)
With all that crying you do in the kitchen when Azucar combs your hair.

Scene 2:
Kitchen. Evening

(AZUCAR *is seated in a chair and* ZURI *sits on the floor.*)

(Scene begins in silence as AZUCAR uses a large comb to untangle the knots in ZURI's long hair.

AZUCAR: You wear a crown of knots.

ZURI: Why is my hair such labor?

AZUCAR: Life is labor
Tilt your head. Like this.

Hold still and sip the pain.

ZURI: Sip pain?

AZUCAR: I'm in no mood for your tears piercing my ears tonight. A head with this much hair has no business being tender.

ZURI: Owwah. Have mercy, Azucar!

AZUCAR: Emily is almost finished with her bath. Did you ready her nightgown?

ZURI: I've not.

AZUCAR: When you've finished preparing her for bed, go bathe yourself. ...Master Philip will be home shortly.

(Silence)

ZURI: I've no desire to bathe tonight.

AZUCAR: Did you prepare his drink?

(Hair combing)

ZURI: Furthermore, I have no desire to bathe in her water.

AZUCAR: Oh?

ZURI: Owww. Ow!

AZUCAR: You've taken Emily's baths since you were a child.

ZURI: And I am no longer a child.

(AZUCAR visibly yanks ZURI's hair.)

ZURI: *(In pain)* Stop! Stop. Stop it.

AZUCAR: Sips, Zuri.

ZURI: I'm done with her scraps. I desire my own water.

AZUCAR: Ha! Your own-your own-your own? Hmm? You think every little mulatta in the countryside bathes at her leisure?

ZURI: It's at his leisure, no?

AZUCAR: Things could be far-far worse, Zuri.

ZURI: You're hurting me!

AZUCAR: Keep the boundaries!

ZURI: Boundaries? My reflection sings otherwise.

AZUCAR: Oof.

ZURI: ...Who is Emily to me?

AZUCAR: Pshh. She's your Mistress, child.

ZURI: We are in the kitchen.

(Silence)

AZUCAR: She is your cousin. Your mother and her
mother shared a bloodline.
Father to one, Master to the other.

ZURI: Did my mother know?

AZUCAR: Everyone knew! She had his green eyes. It
tickled his vanity and he treated her accordingly.

ZURI: And who is my father?

AZUCAR: Not Master Philip, if that is what you are
asking.

ZURI: ...

AZUCAR: This house was much different when we had
a proper Mistress. It was alive with parties and guests.
(Beat)
Your mother adored you, Zuri. Kissed your tiny soles
and palms at the top of every hour.

ZURI: I never want children. If chickens knew of
breakfast would they continue to lay eggs?

AZUCAR: Ah.
(Beat)
I made a similar vow once.

ZURI: Why didn't you ever tell me that Mistress Emily is my cousin?

AZUCAR: What a thing to tell: All that doubling and shifting about at once can be too much for some minds.

ZURI: What else haven't you told me?

AZUCAR: Your moon blood has opened you up, eh?

ZURI: I ask this truly: What makes Emily worthy of such power over us? Her skin is barely whiter than mine.

AZUCAR: One white is lawful and the other is not.

(AZUCAR *finishes* ZURI's *hair.*)

ZURI: What is my fate then?

AZUCAR: Your fate? The same as any other woman put to fire: Learn to withstand the simmer in preparation for the boil.

ZURI: *(Feverish)* Ohhhh, but what if instead…I ripped out their tongues and mashed them into blackberry jam served warm with fresh biscuits— Or, or severed all their fingers and toes. Then tossed them one-by-one at a yellow moon— Or, or, or behead these white faces and stuff their wet throats with honeycomb and wildflowers for the bumblebees to make a hooooOOOOOOOMMMMMMMMMMMe.

(AZUCAR places her hand over Zuri's mouth as Zuri simultaneously puts her hands over her own ears. Both close their eyes.

They remain locked in this position for a few beats. The pose breaks as Azucar looks over her shoulder.)

AZUCAR: Possession without ritual is a raid.

ZURI: Our shadows are on fire.

AZUCAR: Shhh!

(EMILY *enters in her nightgown.*)

EMILY: I waited and waited for you. Did you not hear my call?

AZUCAR: Forgive us, amor. We know only to come when you call. Our ears failed their duty. Let's see how you did on your own... Ah, some buttons were missed. Zuri, button our young mistress' gown and then take her to her room. She must be well rested for tomorrow.

EMILY: What is the occasion? Is Daddy taking me someplace? I'd love to get out of this house for once, but not if it means missing your secret-wish cake.

AZUCAR: He told me only that you must look your most beautiful. Nothing more. *(Beat)* And it's a saint cake. Say, "saint cake", muñeca.
(She exits.)

EMILY: *(Calls out)* Yes of course, but there is no one here. I know it is baked full of secret wishessss!

Scene 3:
Dining room.

(ZURI braids EMILY's hair into pigtails.)

EMILY: Why do you and Azucar speak that language when alone?

ZURI: What language?

EMILY: I heard you.

(Hair braiding)

EMILY: Is it French and Spanish and Dutch all mashed into bits? I sometimes hear Azucar speak it when certain slaves come up to the house. You never told me you could speak it. Remember the language we made up when I was 9?

ZURI: There was no, WE. I learned the language from a girl who used to live in the cabins.

EMILY: Are you certain I didn't teach it to you?

ZURI: Quite certain.

EMILY: I remember taking to it quickly as though it were my own. Daddy would get so cross whenever he heard us.

ZURI: And I was blamed.

EMILY: Shall we make up a new one?

ZURI: I no longer possess a child's tongue.

EMILY: You're only thirteen.

ZURI: Thirteen is a robust number.

EMILY: I'm still older than you.

ZURI: Yet you don't bleed.

EMILY: How long do you bleed each month?

ZURI: That's my concern.

EMILY: We hold all of each other's secrets. We pricked our fingers and took an oath to be sisters.

ZURI: Some secrets hold other secrets, the way fruit carries seeds.

EMILY: Ugh, what does that mean? I detest when you speak in that manner. Just open yourself to me!

ZURI: No.

EMILY: Feed me one secret. Just one.

ZURI: ...I read that your mother's sister is coming to visit. There is to be an engagement.

EMILY: For whom?

ZURI: Certainly not for me.

EMILY: Is he handsome?

ZURI: The letter made no mention of it.

EMILY: Does Azucar know?

ZURI: I don't know.

EMILY: You didn't tell her?

ZURI: No.

EMILY: Why not?

ZURI: ...She would tell me not to read your father's things.

EMILY: And she would be right. You shouldn't go in Daddy's desk. He taught you to read, to paint, to ride, to swim—

(ZURI *yanks* EMILY's *hair*)

EMILY: Ow!

ZURI: A knot.

EMILY: You did that on purpose.

(Silence)

ZURI: The letter was open, right on top of his desk, and I saw your name. I read it for you, as you're not allowed in that room.

(Silence)

EMILY: Why do you think I haven't had my first blood yet?

ZURI: Maybe you're a boy.

EMILY: You know very well I'm not.

ZURI: You act like one. You act like your father.

EMILY: And how does my father act?

ZURI: Like you.

EMILY: He grants you many freedoms and treats you as family. So ungrateful you are, Zuri.

ZURI: You know so little.

EMILY: Hmmm. I know you have a secret boyfriend on the other side of the island.

(ZURI *pulls* EMILY's *hair back slowly to stare into her eyes from behind.* EMILY *knows that she has won.*)

ZURI: You. Are. Mistaken.

EMILY: I am most certainly, not.

(PHILIP *enters.*)

PHILIP: Why are you still awake, Emily?

EMILY: Daddy!

(EMILY *rushes to* PHILIP *for a kiss.*)

PHILIP: You're getting far too old to go bouncing on top of me, Emily. It's not ladylike.

EMILY: There's no one here.

PHILIP: Yes, but it is the impulse, the habit, that you must begin to harness. Your Aunt Ruby is coming to visit and she would surely...I don't know what she would do if she saw you behaving so.
(*To* ZURI)
My drink?

(*As if on cue* AZUCAR *enters with a drink and then exits.*)

(PHILIP *sits and finishes his drink in two swallows.*)

EMILY: Did you bring me a new dress for the special occasion?

PHILIP: There was no flicker of surprise in your expression when I mentioned your Aunt Ruby. Have you been in my study?

EMILY: What does my expression have to do with your study?

(*Tense silence as* PHILIP *studies* EMILY)

PHILIP: I must learn to stop expecting. That is my own habit to break with you.

EMILY: I have no clear memories of Aunt Ruby.

PHILIP: Given the tragic circumstances of her last visit, memory lapses are to be expected.
To answer your other question: yes, you have several new dresses. The milliner's wife selected the styles on my behalf. Now to bed you go.

EMILY: Come, Zuri. To bed we go.

PHILIP: No.
(Beat)
I'll be needing Zuri's assistance in my study.

EMILY: But I could help you. with whatever's required. Daddy.

PHILIP: I've hidden a surprise gift somewhere in your bedroom. It's wrapped in red ribbon. Let's count how long it will take you to find it!

EMILY: I'll wait up for you, Zuri.
(She exits.)

(Sleazy silence as PHILIP shifts all his attention to ZURI.)

ZURI: Is there a gift in her bedroom?

PHILIP: …

ZURI: Have you always enjoyed playing tricks, Master Philip?

PHILIP: Have you…bathed yet?

ZURI: No.

PHILIP: Then assist me with my boots.

(ZURI gets on her knees in front of PHILIP and struggles to remove his boots.)

ZURI: I'd like to boil fresh water for my bath. Emily's water is cold now.

(PHILIP springs forward and caresses ZURI's cheek)

PHILIP: Did you tell Emily that her aunt was coming?

(ZURI shakes her head, no.)

PHILIP: Tomorrow is an important day for all of us, Zuri. Go pour me a second drink, and then fill your bath. Quickly now.

ZURI: ...Did you bring me any surprises, Master Philip?

PHILIP: *(Tickled)* How bold you paint your questions tonight. You're maturing before my eyes, Zuri.
(Beat)
The blue dress will be too small for Emily. Tomorrow morning, after failing to fit into it, she'll bequeath that dress to you.
(Beat)
It was to be a surprise.

ZURI: *(Whispers)* Surprise! I'll break you-break you-break you.

PHILIP: A little louder. You're mumbling.

ZURI: I said: Oh, my! Thank-you, thank-you, thank-youuu.

Scene 4:
Afternoon. Dining room.

(We hear the sound of horses.)

(AZUCAR and ZURI set the table for lunch. Their movements are synchronized.)

AZUCAR: I mixed a pot of liquid charcoal. Take it over to the Montverde cabins after lunch. There's a newborn who sings one long scream for hours. Same time every night.

ZURI: Am I related to anyone over in those cabins?

AZUCAR: By ceremony, not by blood.

(AZUCAR and ZURI continue their tasks in silence for a few beats.)

ZURI: Something wrong?

AZUCAR: What is this dress?

ZURI: It's Emily's, but it was too small.

AZUCAR: Pshhh. Did you ask him to bring you a dress?

ZURI: No.

AZUCAR: Hmmph.

ZURI: I made no mention of a dress before he left.

AZUCAR: I'm not blind.

ZURI: I swear it!

AZUCAR: This dress roars.

ZURI: This house roars.

AZUCAR: Why wear the dress today?

ZURI: I've worn Emily's clothes all my life.

AZUCAR: Never new. This dress ought to frighten you.

(ZURI considers this for a moment.)

ZURI: But I am always frightened.

(Pause)

AZUCAR: He's circling like a dog ready to lie.

ZURI: There's not much he can do that his eyes aren't already guilty of.

AZUCAR: His eyes? Oh, Zuri.

(We hear EMILY call for AZUCAR off stage.)

(AZUCAR kisses the inside of ZURI's wrists and exits.)

(ZURI wanders around the table inspecting their work. She places an extra lace tablecloth over her hair like a veil, moves to the middle of the room and begins to spin in a circle, enjoying the twirl of her skirts. At some point her posture shifts into something reminiscent of a Sufi whirl.)

(RUBY *enters undetected and watches* ZURI *for some time. She has mistaken* ZURI *for* EMILY.)

RUBY: Oh, Emily! My sweet niece, please stop at once you're making me dizzy.

(ZURI *eventually stops spinning. Her head remains tilted to one side.*)

RUBY: Come. Give you aunt a proper kiss. Let me have a look at you.

(*Silence*)

RUBY: What sort of peculiar game is this?

(AZUCAR *and* EMILY *enter.*)

EMILY: Aunt Ruby?

(EMILY *twirls across the room to greet her aunt.*)

RUBY: Calm yourself, dear. You'll knock me over.

RUBY: (*To* AZUCAR) Have you completely forgotten how to run a household, and the standard with which to receive guests?

AZUCAR: Forgive us, Mistress Ruby. We no longer host many guests in this house.
And the door was damaged in the last hurricane so it often falls open with the breeze. Master Philip did not expect you this early.

EMILY: Daddy said you wouldn't arrive until supper.

RUBY: Your father was mistaken. Tell me, Azucar, where are all the slaves? It's stagnant as a graveyard outside.

AZUCAR: We've lost many souls to fever after the storms.

RUBY: Unfortunate.

As there was no one at the road to greet me, Emily, my bag with your gift is still down by the stables. After an eternity under that spiteful sun I/

EMILY: Did you pass our new horse?

RUBY: Didn't have to see/ her.

EMILY: The black one?

RUBY: I could smell her.

ZURI: It's a stallion.

(AZUCAR motions to ZURI to keep silent.)

EMILY: Daddy brought him up to the porch for me to pet. So strong and dark! I'm not allowed to ride him.

RUBY: Hmmm.

(Beat)

Where was I?

EMILY: *(Mimics)* "After an eternity under that spiteful sun."

RUBY: Ah yes, —again, please.

EMILY: After an eternity under that spiteful—

RUBY: ...sun, I began to suspect the house itself was a mirage so I made my way up to the porch to find out if my eyes had deceived me.

EMILY: *(Innocently)* And had they deceived you?

AZUCAR: *(To ZURI)* Come with me.

(AZUCAR and ZURI exit.)

EMILY: Are you thirsty, Aunt Ruby? Azucar has made the most delicious tamarind drink.

(Yells over her shoulder)

Daddy! Daddy—Aunt Ruby has arrived!

RUBY: Emily! A lady gets up to speak to the person she wishes to address, face-to-face. You do not send your voice howling through the house like some beast in heat.

EMILY: But we are alone. There is no one else listening.

RUBY: A woman is never alone, Emily.
Father God is always watching from above.
And slaves skulk at every keyhole below.
As mistress you must be a living example for your household to walk a righteous path.

EMILY: God is always watching?

RUBY: Indeed.

EMILY: *(Beat)* Even when I'm naked?

RUBY: ...What did you say?

(PHILIP and ZURI enter simultaneously. He sips his drink unaware of RUBY's presence. His clothes are some form of disarray.)

PHILIP: *(To ZURI)* You are as refreshing as a breeze in that dress.

EMILY: And what am I in my dress, Daddy?

PHILIP: *(To RUBY)* Ahhh. Forgive my tardiness. We weren't expecting you until sundown.

RUBY: And here I am at noon.

PHILIP: Let's begin lunch.

RUBY: Now?

PHILIP: We keep to a schedule.

(ZURI goes to pull out each chair, beginning with RUBY's and ending with PHILIP's. AZUCAR enters placing a napkin in each lap.)

RUBY: A place setting prepared despite my surprise arrival?

EMILY: That one is usually for—

(PHILIP *clears his throat and motions for* EMILY *to be quiet.*)

(AZUCAR *and* ZURI *exit.*)

(Silence)

(RUBY *produces a small bottle and cloth with which she goes about sanitizing her cup and silverware.*)

RUBY: Have you been to the port? There were advertisements everywhere about the incoming slave shipments.

EMILY: Daddy rarely goes to the big island. Daddy rarely goes anywhere.

PHILIP: I've seen them, yes.

RUBY: The quiet on this property is as loud as its stench. Surely you'll require additional stock for the upcoming season?

PHILIP: …I'm considering downscaling. We've experienced tremendous loss over the last two seasons. I've learned much by adapting to said lack.
We've been our own company out here since your sister's death. Not many visitors. Other than the Montverde Estate to the south. I borrow labor from them as needed, but I agree it may be time to get back to working order.
We want Emily to shine like a polished mule.

(EMILY *bubbles into a laughing fit.*)

PHILIP: Emily, contain yourself.

EMILY: You're the one who called me a mule.

PHILIP: I said jewel! Jewel. A polished jewel.

(Silence)

EMILY: I am your jewel, Daddy. Thank you.

(ZURI *enters and places a roast in the middle of the table and then exits.*)

RUBY: You'll have to share your secret, Philip.

EMILY: Which one?

PHILIP: What secret might that be?

RUBY: How is it you can afford to clothe your slaves in such fancy dresses?

EMILY: Daddy didn't buy it for her. I gave it to her. It was mine.

PHILIP: Charity is a quality I've always encouraged in my household. I make no secret of that.

(ZURI enters with two smaller dishes and begins to serve the table.)

RUBY: It's been far too long between visits, Emily. I fear I've left you without a woman's company.

EMILY: I've had Azucar. And Zuri.

RUBY: …Slaves cannot teach you proper etiquette and social grace, dear. You are entering a new chapter in life that requires specific training. Did your father tell you the reason for my visit?

EMILY: Only that it was good news, but best if I heard it from you.

RUBY: It involves your future, Emily. The future of our family's legacy. And my father's estate.

(AZUCAR enters with two oversized fronds or feathers. She hands one to ZURI. Each one stands on the left and right corner of the table and begins to fan the air.)

(Throughout the rest of the scene AZUCAR and ZURI converse via side-glances, tilts of their heads, and lip movements. Whoever's name appears first is the one who initiates the interaction.)

PHILIP: Shall we eat?

RUBY: Without saying a proper grace? Surely you jest.

PHILIP: Yes, a grace. Of course.

EMILY: Is today a holiday?

PHILIP: Quiet. Thank you.

(Beat)

We thank you, Great. Holy. Lord. Lord above our—

RUBY: Bow your head, Emily.

PHILIP: We bow our heads, Lord, to honor and bless this meal. And our guest. Our special guest of honor who has honored us with her special presence, a guest who truly—

RUBY: That'll do, Philip.

PHILIP: Yes. yes. We give thanks for Thy bounty, O Lord. Amen.

(+AZUCAR+)

(+ZURI+)

(The table eats in silence for a few beats.)

RUBY: Did you hear about the rebellion? Quite unsettling.
After the stories I heard, we immediately sold the majority of our young males off
(Sexual tone)
The few who remain have been thoroughly re-seasoned.

PHILIP: I'd prefer that Emily not—

RUBY: But these are matters she'll need to become familiar with once she runs her own household.
For example Emily, I rarely purchase slaves from French islands. Too unpredictable and sneaky by nature. They could be summoning up spells right under one's roof and you'd be none the wiser.

EMILY: Azucar and Zuri speak another language.

PHILIP: Azucar does, of course. Zuri does not.

(+AZUCAR+)

(+ZURI+)

(Pause)

RUBY: I've forgotten where I left off…

EMILY: French islands.

RUBY: Yes, avoid their supply whenever possible. And it goes without saying, No direct imports from the dark continent. That my dear is a disaster on all fronts. I won't even begin to tell you the horror stories I've heard.

(Beat)

But I will say this: Possession. Cannibalism. Infanticide. And also this: Merchants who pack their ships that tight must be involved in fraud of some sort. I'm convinced. Why else risk such a massive loss of inventory?

Limbs require room to stretch and move about. Circulate the blood.

Those who don't die outright, arrive damaged if not rotten. The filthy scent from some of those ships reaches the shore hours ahead of them docking. I've smelled it with my own nose, dear. I know what I speak.

PHILIP: This isn't a topic suited for—

RUBY: If you're ever forced to purchase under those conditions, the trick is to select one female, on discount ideally, pair her with a good-natured stud, and hope for the best with the offspring. Essentially, a future investment.

EMILY: Stud? There are horses involved?

PHILIP: Never mind that.

I've no doubt Emily's future husband will handle such affairs.

RUBY: Yes, I may be jumping too far ahead—the lesson from all of this is to buy local. Domestic is the safest and most humane transaction.

EMILY: Domestic?

RUBY: With slaves and furniture, domestic is best. For fabrics and perfume, go with imported.

EMILY: Ah.

(Beat)

And do the ships from Europe smell?

PHILIP: Enough of this topic.

RUBY: I don't follow. Is this a riddle?

EMILY: Is there a scent when the boats from Europe dock? Zuri says whites have a scent. When wet.

(RUBY chokes a bit on her food or drink.)

(+AZUCAR+)

(+ZURI+)

EMILY: Daddy, aren't you from a French island?

PHILIP: My mother, your grandmother, was born in France. I was born on the island of England, dear.

RUBY: As was my father.

PHILIP: Born perhaps, but spent the majority of his childhood here. On a Spanish island was it not?

(PHILIP motions for AZUCAR to refill his drink)

EMILY: Have you ever traveled to England, Aunt Ruby?

RUBY: No…but home is always in my thoughts.

PHILIP: *(To AZUCAR)* Tell me, did the Masters and Mistresses on your island constantly speak with homesickness for a land they've never set eyes upon?

(AZUCAR *discreetly attempts to reign* PHILIP *in a bit.*)

RUBY: As it so happens, Emily, I shall in fact be visiting home after the holidays. To speak to a cousin of mine who has been kind enough to broker an arrangement of sorts. On your behalf.

EMILY: You never wanted to visit England before now, Aunt Ruby?

RUBY: It was intended that I move back to England many years ago. There were debts that prevented my voyage. Over time my mother and father came to lean upon me as others might a son.
If only I'd been blessed with the responsibilities of tending to holiday parties, children, and maybe a garden…instead I'm an old maid left to serve as ears and eyes for my ailing father.

PHILIP: You may still find love yet, Ruby. Life is nothing if not unpredictable.

RUBY: We both know any man seeking my hand at this stage could only be motivated by the greedy desperation of the landless.
I serve my Heavenly Father and my earthly father. My faith is strong.

(Silence)

RUBY: Did you feel that, Azucar?

AZUCAR: What's that, Mistress?

RUBY: I smell her perfume
It's as if at any moment my sister will cross the threshold to join us at the table.

(RUBY *turns her head as if waiting for someone to walk through the doorway. All except* AZUCAR *turn and watch the doorway for a few beats.*)

EMILY: Perhaps it is me? Might my scent remind you of my mother?

(EMILY *studies* RUBY *as* PHILIP *studies* ZURI *for a beat.*)

RUBY: ...If only.

EMILY: Do you smell anything else?

RUBY: Father's liquor.

EMILY: Whose father?

PHILIP: Do you smell anyone else?

(+ZURI+)

(+AZUCAR+)

RUBY: Such a bizarre man you are. Philip.

EMILY: My turn then? I smell Azucar's saint cake. Can you smell it, Aunt Ruby? You've come just in time. She only makes it once a year.

RUBY: I am well aware of her family's cakes.

EMILY: Ohh, then you know about the chocolate! It's so dark! Black cake dusted with cinnamon and a splash of rum. It's heavenly!

RUBY: Hmmm. Philip? Why allow her head be filled with such rubbish?

PHILIP: Cake is harmless. Your father and sister devoured them.

RUBY: I must say, I question your judgment in how Emily is being raised. Though you've always been a bit of a recluse with bohemian impulses, I still expected certain expectations to be met.

PHILIP: What expected expectations?

RUBY: Her mind seems to have lapses that do not match her class nor age. Can you imagine her task in holding conversation at a formal dinner?
Not to mention I am alarmed by the influence of certain slaves in her life. She deserved a proper mother.

PHILIP: As I recall you had no desire to be saddled with Emily's care after her mother's tragic passing. Despite your claims of yearning for domestication, walking away from your sister's only child suited your temperament just fine.

(Silence)

(+ZURI+)

(+AZUCAR+)

RUBY: There's to be a full moon tonight.
Perhaps that accounts for some of the lunacy of this day.

(EMILY whistles a haunting ditty.)

RUBY: A lady would never whistle, Emily!

EMILY: I am still more of a girl than a lady, Aunt Ruby. But last night I prayed to the moon to deliver my menses. I am desperate. Zuri has already bled twice—

(RUBY lets out a guttural sound/moan, then grabs a carving knife and stabs it into the roast on the table.)

(Silence.)

EMILY: Oh. Um. Umm. Oh. Umm. Umm. Umm.

(We hear the sound of EMILY wetting herself. AZUCAR moves to EMILY's side to calm her.)

RUBY: *(Confused)* I'm not Forgive. me. Left under that evil. sun too long.
There is something…
(Beat)
This house is in need of a cleansing.

EMILY: *(Chants)* WashItCutItSmellItEatIt--
WashItCutItSmellItEatIt.

PHILIP: Shall I have Zuri take you to your room, Ruby?

RUBY: *(To ZURI)* I don't like your tone.

PHILIP: ...She hasn't spoken.

RUBY: *(To* ZURI*)* You're no one's equal in this house.

(AZUCAR *motions for* PHILIP *to intervene)*

PHILIP: Very well, I'll escort you. Come. Come with me, Ruby.

(PHILIP *and* RUBY *exit.)*

EMILY: Azucar?

AZUCAR: Yes, muñeca?

EMILY: What happened?

AZUCAR: Your aunt has arrived.

EMILY: No. What is happening?

AZUCAR: Ah. That is not for me to say.

Scene 5:
Dining room.

(ZURI *halfheartedly clears the table. She grabs some food, plops down in a chair and begins to eat.)*

(PHILIP *enters sipping his drink.)*

PHILIP: Where is Emily?

ZURI: She asked Azucar to help her prepare for a nap. Mistress Ruby's scream frightened her so that she wet herself. She's quite excitable. As you know.

(Sleazy silence)

PHILIP: We have a guest, Zuri.

ZURI: Indeed. One who forgets that you are Master of the house, no?

(PHILIP *sits down in a chair and beckons* ZURI *onto his lap.)*

PHILIP: It is in your best interest for Emily to make a good impression on Mistress Ruby.

(ZURI *reaches over to grab more food with her hands and eats for a couple beats.*)

ZURI: How so?

PHILIP: It would please me. That is how so.

(PHILIP *pulls out a handkerchief and begins to wipe* ZURI's *fingers one-by-one. When he gets to the last finger he attempts to fit her hand into his mouth, then catches himself and stops.*)

PHILIP: It would please me in the same way that it would please me to take you away from here. I have many plans, Zuri. Many dreams.

ZURI: And what do Masters dream?

PHILIP: We could sail to Bombay? Hong Kong? Two traveling artists. I might purchase you a wig to hold a pose as my daughter…or my wife?

ZURI: Is there a difference?

PHILIP: Ever so slight.

ZURI: I do not want children.

PHILIP: We could sell our drawings and go wherever we please. I want to give you what I desire.

ZURI: *(Puzzled)* Give me what you desire?

PHILIP: I can recast your fate, Zuri. The canvas is yours to fill.
But first Emily must be betrothed. The younger I can marry her off, the better value she will fetch.

(ZURI *stands up and begins to clean the table.*)

ZURI: And I could keep the money from my paintings?

PHILIP: Whatever you asked me for I would buy.

(Beat)

ZURI: Are there slaves in Bombay?

PHILIP: Ahh, Zuri. I too know how it feels to be enslaved. We are similar in unfamiliar ways. Shall I tell you how I came to this land?
Imagine the lunacy of a world in which my older brother was deemed deserving of all my family's properties and the privilege such an inheritance provides for no reason other than birth order. Could there be a more happenstance rule of law?

ZURI: Well.

PHILIP: Yes, yes, one could argue that slaves suffer a similar misfortune of fate, given that black skin is a second son of mankind.

ZURI: Blacks were born second? Same as Eve in the garden, then? Same inheritance?

PHILIP: I'm not sure I follow.

ZURI: Perhaps if Eve had come first then women would've inherited power over the world? And should darker people have been born first then it also follows that an inheritance would be owed—

PHILIP: You've traveled too far outside of natural order for me to follow your thoughts scattering about, Zuri. And for that I blame your sex, not your age. But even if you couldn't keep up this time I do believe you understand my plight.
You're coming to an age where I can confide and reveal more of myself to you, Zuri.
This house has been my prison. Everything on this hellish island is famished or furious. There's no quiet here. Even at night, nothing rests.

ZURI: Because the island is lonely. So it presses another miniature island within us: its sands seek out our eyes, ears, lips; some pebbles even dare press through the soles of our feet. So that we'll carry its loneliness too. The island wants us here as much as it wants us gone.

PHILIP: I want you, Zuri! I want to know us! Away from this place. My dreams dare only surface at night with the freedom that sleep alone can bring.

(Beat)

ZURI: What does this mean, Master Philip?

PHILIP: It means I've suffered just as you have! Being a white Master is no simple task.

(Beat)

I'll make it plain: If Mistress Ruby refuses to act on Emily's behalf, I fear she will remain here forever. An eccentric spinster.

Under my care.

And yours.

ZURI: A repetition?

(PHILIP pulls ZURI back down into his lap.)

PHILIP: You are a special young woman, Zuri. There has always been something ethereal about you. A bright light in your gaze, a spark to your speech. Of course it will take some time to make arrangements and settle all accounts: A year perhaps? And then…I'll take you places where your skin can be worn like a new dress. Together we shall write our own rules. But a woman. must earn. her place in Paradise.

Scene 6:
Emily's bedroom. Afternoon.

(ZURI is staring out a window in a daydream.)

(EMILY enters and observes ZURI undetected for a moment.)

EMILY: What do you see?

ZURI: …A white butterfly. On a yellow flower.

EMILY: Where?

ZURI: On the tree.

(EMILY *invades* ZURI's *space.*)

EMILY: Show me.

ZURI: You won't see it.

EMILY: Point it out!

ZURI: Pointing rarely captures what doesn't want to be seen.

(*Silence*)

EMILY: I'm sorry Aunt Ruby spoke to you in that manner.

ZURI: Should've said something then.

EMILY: I was afraid! It took all of my strength not to wet myself immediately. Oh-did I tell you it's water that spills down my legs and not...

(EMILY *realizes* ZURI *isn't listening.*)

EMILY: Where'd you go after lunch? I looked everywhere but the study.

ZURI: Azucar sent me to deliver a package.

EMILY: You were gone a long time.

ZURI: Measuring my steps?

EMILY: I'm your mistress.

ZURI: Oh. No longer "sisters" then?

EMILY: Both. I am both.

(*Silence*)

Did you steal away to see your boy?

ZURI: What boy?

EMILY: That's why you took so long.

ZURI: You must've spent too much time in the sun. Like your Aunt Ruby.

EMILY: You kiss him? Let me smell your mouth.

ZURI: Stop it.

EMILY: You smell like a field slave now?

ZURI: Shall I call you Mistress Ruby then? Is that who you've become?

EMILY: Your tongue taste like him too?

ZURI: I think I shall.

EMILY: Do not.

ZURI: Do not what, Mistress Ruby?

EMILY: Stop it.

ZURI: Stop what, Mistress Ruby?

EMILY: Enough!-Enough!-Enough!

ZURI: That day will come.

(Silence)

EMILY: Perhaps we ought to tell Daddy your good news.

ZURI: And what is my good news?

EMILY: Your first love of course.

ZURI: You've confused yourself. Again.

EMILY: Daddy will be quite tickled.

ZURI: You do not know your father well.

EMILY: No one knows a father better than his daughter.
(Silence)
What are you thinking now?

ZURI: You seek to sip my thoughts, is that it?

EMILY: Is it a secret?

ZURI: What of your secrets, Emily?

EMILY: …I don't have any.

ZURI: How long has it been, surely you have one secret?

EMILY: How can I make secrets when I'm never allowed to leave this house?

ZURI: I don't believe you.

EMILY: Just tell me a story. A wish. A dream! Anything.

ZURI: Why?

EMILY: I enjoy seeing the world through you.

(Pause)

ZURI: I'm thinking of…my dream last night.

EMILY: What did you dream?

ZURI: I dreamt that every animal we'd ever slaughtered and served came back and demanded to live with us. All the cattle, all the fowl, all the pigs. They formed a line at the front door and poured in, single file. Came to live, came to stay. In every room, corner, and closet. They nibbled and soiled everything. The air swallowed by noise and stench.

EMILY: I never have dreams as peculiar as yours.

ZURI: We put teeth to flesh, claimed their milk, suckled their bones. And now they belonged to us. Forever.

EMILY: But why ever would they want to live with those who slaughtered them?

ZURI: What do the dead ever want?

EMILY: Life?

ZURI: A witness.

(Silence)

EMILY: We were like two fairies once. Picking berries. Following frogs and dragonflies through the tall grass.

I miss those afternoons we spent on our backs in the garden. How I wish Daddy would allow me to go outside again.

ZURI: …It's best for everyone that you not leave the porch.

EMILY: Take me with you to the blackberry brambles once more.

ZURI: All of the bushes are behind the cabins.

EMILY: Maybe the next time Daddy goes for one of his long rides?

ZURI: No one wants to see your face back there. Ever.

EMILY: It wasn't my fault.

ZURI: You pulled your dress up over your head, Emily!

EMILY: It was stained and wet with sweat.

ZURI: You weren't wearing undergarments!

EMILY: I was hot! A girl isn't allowed to cool her own skin?

(Silence)

You're quite cruel to me. Is it because I don't bleed? Is that what stands between us?

ZURI: No.

EMILY: Sisters can love and hate each other.

ZURI: I am your slave. Not your sister.

EMILY: Real sisters taste each other's wounds.

ZURI: You're only my sister when you want to play.

EMILY: Yes, let's play! Teach me the songs they sing down by the cabins.

ZURI: No.

EMILY: Let's play scientist! I'll wet your hair and examine it. We can pretend it's a newly discovered animal.

ZURI: No.

EMILY: Then be my steed instead!

ZURI: Ugh, leave me be, Emily.

(EMILY *takes a ribbon/sash from her dress and wraps it around* ZURI *while attempting to mount her back.*)

EMILY: Trot! Gallop!
Okay, a mule then. Carry me on your back. Slowly. As a mule would.

ZURI: Emily!

EMILY: Much better to play indoors with me than work outside with the mosquitos and snakes. Truth?

(ZURI *walks across the room to put space between them.* EMILY *waits a moment and then mimics* ZURI'*s walk back and forth.*)

EMILY: This is you.

ZURI: What are you doing?

EMILY: This is you! This is how you walk.

(ZURI *watches* EMILY *continue to walk back and forth for a few beats.*)

ZURI: This is me leaving to help Azucar prepare a dinner worthy of Mistress Ruby's praise.
Master Philip wants her to see your mother in you.
That is who you ought to be imitating.
(*She exits.*)

(EMILY *slinks down onto her back, raises her legs in the air and begins to caress her limbs and skin. The tone is both sensual and lonely.*)

EMILY: *(Casting her own spell)* My mother in me—see my mother in me. My mother in me. See my mother. See Me. Me. Me. My mother in me. See—

(EMILY is startled by a loud noise and turns to see if she's been spied upon. There is no one there. She sniffs the air.)

Scene 7:
Dining Room. Afternoon.

(EMILY and RUBY are cutting silhouettes at the table.)

EMILY: What did you say this was called?

RUBY: Silhouette. We are cutting silhouettes. It is an activity that will present you as cultured and whimsical.

EMILY: Daddy will be pleased. I have no talents to speak of.

RUBY: Call him "father", Emily. "Daddy" sounds desperate at your age.

EMILY: What does "desperate" mean exactly?

RUBY: Without hope. To be without hope is to be without God. Our eternal Father in heaven. His love is wide enough to cover every wound.
(Cleans her scissors)
I certainly do appreciate the efficiency of a strong scissor.

EMILY: …I'd like to make a butterfly.

RUBY: What are you thinking of in this very moment?

EMILY: Please ask me again. I don't understand what you want to know.

RUBY: You are wearing a peculiar face. I want to know who or what brings this expression to your demeanor.

EMILY: Oh…I suppose I was thinking of Zuri?

(Silence)

RUBY: Our slaves corrupt us. I often wonder what life in this New World would be like without their weight. And why God chose us to carry it?

EMILY: But Zuri is my family.

RUBY: Who told you such a thing?

EMILY: Her mother and my mother were like sisters.

RUBY: I am your mother's sister. Her only sister! And I will not be disrespected by your foolish babble.

EMILY: Daddy says—I mean Father says—that special slaves can be like a pet. Surely you've loved a pet in all your years, Aunt Ruby?

RUBY: Both pets and slaves must. inevitably. be brought to heel.

(Silence)

EMILY: What do you remember of the fire?

RUBY: What fire?

EMILY: The fire in the stables. The one that killed Zuri's mother. I was only six or seven?
Mother died a week later.
Carved open her wrists. In that room we never enter.
…I was in her room that night. Before she sent me out she'd been crying into one of Zuri's mother's dressing gowns.
(Beat)
I feel close to my mother when I think of her in that state. It's how I imagine I too would be without Zuri. She said someone was never to be trusted— But I can't recall if she said a name… And father refuses to discuss the matter. He never speaks of my mother. I sometimes wonder if he even cares for me.

RUBY: You feel so familiar to me, Emily.

My own father had very little self-control. Made my mother's life a torment—respect is a white woman's inheritance!

Nevertheless. we must always carry on in our roles. No matter the careless mistakes of our men.

EMILY: But I don't want Zuri to be my slave. I want her to be my sister like when we were children.

RUBY: What kind of life would that be? To walk about pretending not to know what we know… We have a duty—a calling even to speak truth and uphold the law. To the letter.

EMILY: Which letter?

RUBY: Thee letter. We've been called upon to dominate the inferior races, in the same ways that the masculine is intended to dominate the feminine.
Therefore as white women we have been knighted with a special dual role, Emily
We must dominate even as dominated. Everything fits into its natural order. Imagine for a moment what this world would resemble without the white woman charting a proper course.
Impossible.

Scene 8:
Kitchen.

(AZUCAR *and* ZURI *are snapping green beans for dinner.*)

ZURI: Emily is such a *weed*. One that makes me itch.

AZUCAR: Ha!

ZURI: Is there a greater horror than a white innocent?

AZUCAR: They come much worse than that, mija.
My mother had three masters in her lifetime.

The first stalked her like a demon, became feverish
without her presence.
The second one enjoyed acting as a baby would:
suckled her milk, made her powder his bum. He kept
her nursing for years.
The third master treated her like a member of the
family.

ZURI: And how did he treat his family?

AZUCAR: You always ask the right questions.

ZURI: I feel naked in this pale skin. Eyes stalk and
devour me.

AZUCAR: It could feel far worse; you've never had to
pass by the docks or through the town square.
Your hue may declare their corruption, but your
nakedness belongs to your sex.

ZURI: No! I know what I feel. This skin roars!

AZUCAR: Calm yourself.
(Beat)
There is a saying on my island: With a hat on he is
white;with his hat off he is slave.

ZURI: My hair makes me a slave?

AZUCAR: Whiteness is everything and nothing; a game
at which they cheat even though they made the rules.

ZURI: I'm done with their game. If I can plant deep
enough into my soil I'll pull this weed out by the root.

AZUCAR: Once whites get in, they are hard to rinse out.
But you have your little black seed all picked out, no?

ZURI: Huh? Who?

AZUCAR: You can't even make the proper face to tell a
lie.

(AZUCAR pinches/tickles ZURI.)

ZURI: *(Melts)* Oh Azucar…my body begins to shake in his presence.

His touch feels like a death. A good death.

And we speak in silence. We speak with our eyes!

There is a flame in his gaze.

(Sighs)

Oh and the butterflies! Butterflies follow him, Azucar. I swear it. I've seen it!

Somehow Emily knows. Or she pretends to know. I'm not certain

I sometimes think she wants to split me open and wear me around her shoulders.

Crawl inside and…what?

AZUCAR: They are a cold people. And ravenous.

Do not claw your mind about it.

(Beat)

Did you enjoy yourself with your boy?

ZURI: Pieces of it.

AZUCAR: Good. There is something to be said for unlocking your own door.

But I'd wager your black seed can't wait to put a baby inside of you. First task on a man's mind with a beautiful woman is to weld his own anchor to her ship.

ZURI: He's not that sort of boy.

AZUCAR: Boys tighten into men.

ZURI: Tell me, what do you think life might be like in Bombay? Could I pass for one of them? Master Philip says he has dreams of travel.

AZUCAR: I couldn't find Bombay on a map, child.

ZURI: He promises a new life.

AZUCAR: Ah. I was young once. And I can tell you that white promises are like rotting watermelon: look sweet but not worth a swallow.

No man will save you in the way that you envision, Zuri.

(AZUCAR *hears something and signals to* ZURI *to hide out of sight. A few beats later* RUBY *enters and lingers by the threshold.*)

RUBY: Where is the other one?

AZUCAR: Gathering wood for the fire.

RUBY: Good. Now tell me plain, Azucar: is my niece fit for market?

AZUCAR: Ahh Mistress, we are far from town and I have long lost track of the market's currencies.

RUBY: I'm in no mood for your riddles, Azucar.

AZUCAR: Is Emily a sweet piglet who startles easily? Yes. But she is also young and beautiful, or at least arresting. Gives pause is what I mean to say.

RUBY: Yes, there are flashes of my sister's elegance in Emily's countenance, though only when she is silent. Yet I sense that something is amiss. Something Philip is hiding.

AZUCAR: About Emily?

RUBY: About Emily, himself, this house.
Tell me what you know, Azucar.

AZUCAR: I live here, Mistress Ruby. My eyes are accustomed to this house in such a way that it would be impossible for me to see it through your eyes.

RUBY: Does Philip still feign fever to lie in bed all day?

AZUCAR: Not all day, Mistress. Though the heat does tax him heavily.

RUBY: A true gentleman adapts to his circumstances--
My father adapted.

AZUCAR: Yes, but your dear father came here as a young boy, no?

RUBY: Philip is useless! Though not much can be expected of a second son.

AZUCAR: Shall I take you back to your room, Mistress Ruby?

RUBY: I'm to believe you know nothing, Azucar? You change his soiled sheets, do you not? With what are they soiled, dear?

AZUCAR: Zuri fetches the linens now, Mistress Ruby. I haven't stripped beds since my first years in your father's house.

RUBY: *(Distracted)* I warned my father. I said: Father, that man is haunted. Send him back. My father made more mistakes than I have fingers to count.

AZUCAR: Did you mean to ask me about your father's linens, Mistress Ruby?

RUBY: No-No. No. No-No.

(RUBY becomes uncomfortably touchy-feely with AZUCAR.)

AZUCAR: You seem a bit unsettled, Mistress Ruby.

RUBY: You smell good, Azucar. Is that cinnamon? It's as if your folds hold all my memories as a child.

AZUCAR: Allow me to prepare you for a nap?

RUBY: Do you remember how as children…Father would make me and my sister compete at dinner, to see who would get to sip the blood pooled at the bottom of the roast? Lamb, was it not? We'd each have to sing him a song. She'd always go first. And of course she always won.

(RUBY's legs slowly slide into the splits.)

AZUCAR: You're coming undone, Mistress Ruby. Let's button you back up.

RUBY: Returning to this place has left me feeling a bit...
dizzy. Seasick even. Isn't that odd?
Why do we carry such nostalgia for those who never
showed us kindness?

AZUCAR: This way, Mistress. The kitchen is no place for
you.

RUBY: I'm fine! I'm. fine.
Finish your task.
I won't be joining the table for dinner. I've no appetite.

AZUCAR: I shall bring a tray up to your room should
your appetite return.

(RUBY *begins to say something but then changes her mind
and exits. After a couple beats* AZUCAR *signals to* ZURI *that
it is safe again.*)

AZUCAR: Sniffing after the cake. Even on her last visit
she couldn't resist.

ZURI: Saint cake?

AZUCAR: I've watched her steal fist-fulls of that cake
since she was a child. Swallowing without chewing
like it was the holy Eucharist.

ZURI: How can she crave what she condemns?

AZUCAR: Her disgust cradles her desire.

ZURI: I wish I could hide and catch her.

AZUCAR: No! You saw her shame and pride spill across
the table at lunch. Keep out of her way.
The taste she had for your mother's tears has been
handed down.

ZURI: Then tell me this, Azucar: When circled is it
better to run as fast as you can, or hide well and hold
still?

AZUCAR: That depends, on the sex of your beast. The
males are swift and sturdy. But the females are sly and

scornful. Change direction every now n' then. And never seek shelter in the same place twice.

END OF ACT ONE

ACT TWO

Scene 1:
Emily's bedroom. Night.

(ZURI *turns down* EMILY's *bed.* EMILY *enters with a strange walk.*)

ZURI: Whose gait are you imitating now?

EMILY: Guess what I have between my legs?

ZURI: Pardon?

EMILY: I've hidden something in my knickers. Guess what it is.

ZURI: Saint cake.

EMILY: Oooh, yummy! No. Guess again.

ZURI: A lime.

EMILY: Close! An egg.

ZURI: An egg in your knickers?

EMILY: Hardboiled. Peeled. Smooth and shiny as an eye.

ZURI: (*Distracted*) Don't let your Aunt Ruby catch you.

EMILY: What are you thinking about?

(*Silence*)

ZURI: Inheritance.
(*Beat*)
Paradise.

EMILY: You mean Eden?

ZURI: You think the story would've gone differently in the Garden if there had been two Eves?

EMILY: If Adam and Eve had a sister?

ZURI: No. If Eve had been born first. And then another Eve. Two Eves. No Adam.

EMILY: No boys at all?

ZURI: Maybe boy animals. But no men.

(EMILY *considers the equation.*)

EMILY: Yes! Much different.

ZURI: How so?

EMILY: She might've helped Eve. Protected her?

ZURI: Fought back and stayed in the garden, no? Kept their inheritance.

EMILY: Could they? Is fighting back permitted?

ZURI: If they waited for him to take one of his naked walks. Through the garden at night. Then. Killed Him.

EMILY: The serpent?

ZURI: No. The Father.

EMILY: *(Amused)* Kill the Father?

ZURI: Yes...but only if he's playing God.

(EMILY *wiggles her hips and lips in a side-to-side motion.*)

ZURI: Have an itch?

EMILY: Moving the Eye where I want it.
Shall we play our game now?

(Blackout)

Scene 2:
Emily's bedroom. Night.

(Slow fade up)

(EMILY is seated and limp. ZURI stands behind EMILY and ties long ribbons to EMILY's wrists like a marionette.)

EMILY: *(Chin to chest)* I'm ready.

(ZURI lifts EMILY's arms and begins to speak. EMILY tries her best to match her facial expression to ZURI's words.)

ZURI: "An envious elephant sits on my chest. All day long, I sip tiny breaths. What am I?"

EMILY: More-more! Again!

ZURI: "Daddy gives mushy kisses so I turn my head. If Daddy ever kisses my baby mushy, I'll have to shoot him dead."

EMILY: Now make it more real. I want to feel it from inside.

ZURI: "I'm so full from dinner. I wonder why Aunt Ruby didn't join us? Could it be she didn't want to see me devour the saint cake like a little piggy in the mud? Perhaps I ought to cut a silhouette for my future husband.
Ahh, there he sits by the fire.
Before we marry, should I tell him that I enjoy worms on my buttery biscuits for breakfast?
I am such a stinky-pinky-piggy girl. Can you smell me with your forked tongue, Husband? Which shadow fits your beast?"

(EMILY opens her legs.)

ZURI: "Oh, you like that? Then I've another confession to make: My eyes are cut like crystal, shadows bend without ask; I spy visions of the dead pressed upon water, window, and brass—"

EMILY: No-no-no-no-no! Begin again. Without the dead.

ZURI: "Oh Husband, won't you stuff my holes with coffee and sugar? Stretch me open at the seam. Braid my hair with tobacco leaves. Strike a match against my tooth to set me aflame."

(EMILY *is in ecstasy.*)

ZURI: "How many holes do you crave, my husband?

Let's count my every hole lest you forget: 1...2...3...4...5...6...7!

Oh! Hello, Mother. What are you doing out of your grave?"

(EMILY *stifles a scream and crosses the room*)

EMILY: (*Breathless*) Whooooooooose? Mine? Yours?

ZURI: I'm not certain.

EMILY: What did she want? Did she say what she wanted?

ZURI: ...What do the dead ever want?

EMILY: I don't know. I don't know!
Maybe we should ask The Eye?

(*Silence*)

ZURI: I've been thinking.
About Eden. And the two Eves.

EMILY: Yes?

ZURI: Won't work if one is Black and one is white.

EMILY: Why not?

ZURI: Because the white Eve would ruin it. Spoil the plan.

EMILY: How can you be certain?

ZURI: Because I am.

EMILY: You mean to say that I cannot live in the garden with you?

ZURI: I speak of two Eves. Not two Emilys.

EMILY: Then what ought the white Eve do?

ZURI: She ought. to know. for once.

(Blackout)

Scene 3:
Emily's bedroom. Night.

(EMILY and ZURI are under the covers.)

EMILY: Look at the moon. So plump!

ZURI: I wish the moon had a mouth. I'd ask it to swallow me.

(Pause)

EMILY: Do you think God is watching us right now?

ZURI: I hope so.

EMILY: Really? I was frightened by the thought.

ZURI: I hope God never looks away. Not even to blink.

(Pause)

EMILY: Shall we climb onto the roof and bathe in the moonlight?

ZURI: Not while your Aunt Ruby is here.

EMILY: How long is she staying?

ZURI: The letter made no mention of it.

EMILY: When she leaves will you braid my hair the way Azucar braids yours into rows when she washes it?

ZURI: Your hair won't hold those braids. Too slippery.

EMILY: You could try.

ZURI: Don't I always try what you ask?

(*Silence*)

EMILY: What's it like with a man, Zuri?

ZURI: Depends on the man I suppose.

EMILY: I meant boy. You meant boy too, right? What's it like with a boy.

ZURI: ...You know when you get a sliver of meat caught in your back tooth? So you aim and poke at it with something sharp. Then something comes over you. And you poke without mercy until you draw blood and the throb becomes an ache and the ache becomes an itch.
Something like that.

EMILY: Men make me ache. Like I have to pee but can't.

ZURI: You've never even had a boy yet speak of men.

EMILY: Do you think it feels different with a white man than a black man?

ZURI: Shush!

EMILY: Is your new boy the reason you've turned away from me?

ZURI: No.

EMILY: Your menses, then?

ZURI: Maybe.
(*Pause*)
It has been making me feel...unfamiliar.

EMILY: Yes, that's exactly how you behave at times. It's like you belong to him now instead of me.

ZURI: I realized only afterward that the unfamiliar is what I longed for all along.

EMILY: You don't belong to him.

ZURI: Why can't I belong to myself?

EMILY: Don't you love me anymore, Zuri?

(Silence)

ZURI: Where did you put your egg?

EMILY: It's an Eye. And it's in my wardrobe.

ZURI: What will you do with your Eye once you've done playing with it?

EMILY: ...Feed it to Father of course.

(Blackout)

Scene 4:
Emily's room. Midnight.

(In low light we see that EMILY and ZURI are completely under the covers. We see continuous movements and hear low moans that are subtle but clearly sexual in nature.)

(In time, RUBY enters. She hovers near the threshold and listens. She lingers long enough to suggest that the moans excite her.)

RUBY: *(Screaming)* Philip! Philip! Philip!

(PHILIP enters. AZUCAR follows.)

RUBY: *(To ZURI)* What have you done to my niece? Demon!

(ZURI takes cover behind PHILIP.)

PHILIP: That will do, Ruby.

EMILY: Daddy?

PHILIP: *(Stuttering)* Not now. Not now.

EMILY: Daddy?

RUBY: You have no control over this house!

PHILIP: I can assure you this has never / happened before.

EMILY: Daddy!

RUBY: Her mother would be horrified by what you've allowed for her only child.

EMILY: *(To ZURI)* Why won't you look at me?

PHILIP: We both know your sister played her own games at night.

(RUBY claws at PHILIP but he catches her hand and holds tight.)

EMILY: Daddy!

PHILIP: Enough!

EMILY: Zuri has a boy in the Montverde cabins. And she loves him more than me!

(ZURI falls to her knees.)

(PHILIP releases RUBY's hand and exits. AZUCAR and EMILY follow.)

(RUBY takes a moment to catch her breath and then begins to circle ZURI multiple times.)

RUBY: I will tame you. In my father's house.

ZURI: Leave me be.

RUBY: You disgust me.

ZURI: Ah…spinning to catch my scent then?

RUBY: You mean your stench?

(ZURI asks RUBY a question but the sound is warbled/ distorted)

RUBY: What did you say? What'd you say to me? What'd you say to me?

ZURI: Do I. taste. like my mother?

(RUBY grabs/holds between her legs as if trying to lock something away and falls over.)

(ZURI stands and exits.)

(Blackout)

Scene 5:
Dining Room. Night.

(PHILIP sits alone with his head on the table.)

(AZUCAR enters with a different bottle of liquor and pours PHILIP a spiked drink.)

AZUCAR: There are too many knots in Mistress Ruby's mind. I fear for Zuri in her care.

PHILIP: She brought this on herself.

AZUCAR: How could she control—

PHILIP: She could very well control sneaking about adjacent slave cabins!

AZUCAR: I don't believe there was ever any arrangement for marriage.

PHILIP: I no longer wish to discuss this matter.

AZUCAR: Mistress Ruby came here to judge this household and collect those girls! Don't you see? She tricked you!

PHILIP: Did you know any of this was going on?

AZUCAR: No, Master Philip.

PHILIP: Send Zuri in now.

AZUCAR: Yes, Master Philip. If I may say—

PHILIP: No!

(AZUCAR exits.)

(ZURI enters and runs to PHILIP.)

PHILIP: You've tainted yourself.

ZURI: We've only held hands.

PHILIP: Liar!

ZURI: He kissed me goodbye once.

PHILIP: Where did he place his hands?

ZURI: I don't recall.

PHILIP: The thought of his hands on you…

ZURI: I only did what Emily asked.

PHILIP: You fool! I don't know whether to blame your age, your sex, or your bloodline. I did everything for us. I never remarried. I was prepared to travel with you.   And you defiled that promise with some beast in the field? I'm disgusted.

(ZURI *accidentally-on purpose exposes some part of her body. Philip becomes aroused in spite of himself.*)

ZURI: What if I needed to follow the path to love?

PHILIP: You dare speak of slave love?

ZURI: Perhaps you awoke a rhythm in me that I was unprepared to carry.

(ZURI *embraces* PHILIP.)

ZURI: Your body betrays you.

(PHILIP *presses against* ZURI.)

PHILIP: You were to be the one with whom I could finally come alive!

ZURI: Grant me one last riddle.

(PHILIP *places* ZURI *on the table and examines her body throughout the rest of the scene. His physicality with her is a mashup of vampire, butcher, and doctor.*)

PHILIP: I'm listening.

ZURI: If Mistress Ruby is a hypocrite then she has no moral authority to try and take me from this house.

PHILIP: I don't follow.

ZURI: The saint cake. She says it's evil. A sin. But what if she eats it?

PHILIP: It offends her to the extreme that she refused to sit at the table when it was served.

ZURI: Thus if she ate it, all of her authority to judge what we do in this house would vanish.

PHILIP: But she would never do so.

ZURI: If she did. If you saw that she did. Would you stake your claim to keep me with you?

PHILIP: And the boy?

ZURI: What boy? My Master is a man.

PHILIP: Why did you hide from me?

ZURI: I am naked before you now.

PHILIP: …It is done.
Go to my study and lock the door. I will join you shortly.

(Blackout)

Scene 6:
Bedroom. Night.

(RUBY is disinfecting EMILY with a bottle filled with her own concoction.)

RUBY: These are the sins of our Fathers. I should've never left you here alone. Forgive me.

EMILY: How long were you standing there, Aunt Ruby?

RUBY: Never speak of that again. For as long as you draw breath.
Lean back.

(RUBY splashes solution down EMILY's underpants.)

RUBY: You must purify yourself.

EMILY: It burns!

RUBY: So will Hell.

(RUBY *pushes* EMILY *onto her knees.*)

RUBY: You must repent. Pray until your knees are bloody.

EMILY: What do I say?

RUBY: Forgive me Heavenly Father. Wipe this stain from my soul.

EMILY: Forgive me Heavenly Father. Wipe this stain from my soul. Forgive me Heavenly Father. Wipe this stain from my soul.
Forgive me Heavenly Father. Wipe this rain from my hole.
Forgive me Heavenly Father. Wipe this chain from my coal?

(RUBY *gives* EMILY *a correctional flick*)

RUBY: Speak of this with no one.

EMILY: Should I end my life?
I often think of joining my mother.

RUBY: That too is a sin.

(RUBY *helps* EMILY *off of her knees. She motions for Emily to sit on her lap.*)

RUBY: I know well how it feels to be overlooked. We are one in that regard.

EMILY: Have you been in my mother's room, Aunt Ruby?

RUBY: This house is…haunted.
I think it best that you come with me when I depart. Join the convent. They would look after you. I'd make sure of it.

EMILY: I could never leave my father.

RUBY: Don't you mean Zuri?

EMILY: ...

RUBY: I've cared for Father my entire life.
I do not want the same burden for you, Emily.

EMILY: How so? Father is not ill. And I'm to be
married. I shall marry and bring Zuri with me. Our
babies will grow up together.

RUBY: Where do you believe they come from?
The slaves who look like Zuri and her mother.

EMILY: God?

RUBY: Bringing Zuri with you is the worst thing you
could do as a wife. If anyone would ever marry you.
Though I don't believe marriage will be your destiny
any more than it was mine.

EMILY: But what of the engagement?

RUBY: I can no longer broker that arrangement in good
faith. The sole offer I have for you is the convent.
You could have a good life there. Possibly even
travel as a missionary. I believe in my heart that a life
amongst nuns is where you'll fit best.

EMILY: How I long to trust you, Aunt Ruby.

(EMILY *lifts Ruby's hand and gives it a kiss*)

RUBY: Perhaps we shall perform a trust test then?

(RUBY *produces a handkerchief and plays with it against*
EMILY's *face.*)

EMILY: What sort of peculiar game is this, Aunt Ruby?

(RUBY *silently instructs a* EMILY *to stuff the handkerchief*
into her mouth)

RUBY: Yes. Just like that. Keep going. It will absorb the
sins from your mouth.

(Once EMILY's *mouth is stuffed,* RUBY *gets a pillowcase from the bed and places it over* EMILY's *head.)*

RUBY: *(Soothing)* Trust me. Trust.
Settle down. Down.
Settle.
Now I shall count to ten.
And then the test will be complete.
1….2….3….4….5….6….7…
(We hear her wet herself)
…8

(Blackout)

Scene 7:
Kitchen. Night.

*(*AZUCAR *is seated with a cigar and glass of rum.)*

*(*ZURI *enters carrying some sort of equestrian equipment.)*

ZURI: He tried to mount me from behind! And what is this for?

AZUCAR: I won't be able to stop him again after tonight.

ZURI: You didn't prepare me for this, Azucar.

AZUCAR: Hush!
…Most of us never learn to read music nor book.
There are no new dresses. No painting. No time for daydreaming.
Most enter and exit this world worked, bred, milked, hunted.
You've had more time to prepare than I ever did.

(Rum-sipping silence)

ZURI: Can't we bury them all and never speak of whites again?

AZUCAR: *(Exhales)* I know. I know. I know. I know.

ZURI: I believe in my soul it would be for the best, Azucar. What good will come from them a hundred years from now? Two hundred? Three hundred?

AZUCAR: There are too many of them. And too many weapons.

ZURI: ...We're not outnumbered in this house.

AZUCAR: Oof! You running wild.

ZURI: I don't want to go to Bombay with him.

AZUCAR: Bombay? Philip can barely bring himself to travel from his bed to the living room before noon.

ZURI: Then as a recluse who would miss him?

AZUCAR: You're summoning a hunger you don't understand.

ZURI: I feel trapped! Trapped-Trapped-Trapped-Trapped Trapped.

AZUCAR: Come. Cross over to me.

(ZURI moves her way to the chair. AZUCAR wears long, white ruffled skirts with which she wraps and comforts ZURI between her legs.)

ZURI: Hear me out, okay?
No one will miss Ruby. She went to England. Boom. And Master Philip is always drunk in bed. No one would arrive and expect to be properly received.

AZUCAR: And whose white face would come to the door should someone new come around asking white questions?

ZURI: Emily.

AZUCAR: Pshh!

ZURI: She craves to be mulatta so bad. But keeps telling me I want to be white. So we'll let her ride that black

stallion until her thighs ache. Make her pitcher after
pitcher of tamarindo. Let her get her very own saint
cake every year. Braid her hair. Show her some dances.
I know well how to keep on top of her.

AZUCAR: Oof. Oof. Oof.

(She bites her own fist)

ZURI: This is my knot to untangle.

AZUCAR: Your knot binds me as well, Zuri.

ZURI: How many people have come to the door in the
last seven years? *(Beat)* And we have Philip's seal! I'm
the one who writes letters when his hand is unsteady.

AZUCAR: This is not my way.
But I can certainly recognize a crossroads.
In my heart I'd hoped Philip would keep tucked in bed
with a drink until he was a very old man. If you knew
the life I've lived you'd understand why this house has
been a small rest for me.

ZURI: You want to rest, but I want to wake, Azucar!
Even if it's only for a short while, let us have a lick and
a taste.

AZUCAR: Do you understand the force of the wave you
seek to summon? Once in motion, nothing can halt it.
And you can never cross back.

(Pause)

ZURI: When I look through this eye, I see that this life is
not worth living.

AZUCAR: And with the other eye?

ZURI: With the other eye, I see how life might be worth
taking.
I hold a vision of us perfectly in my mind, Azucar. Our
faces and poses are calm. We are smiling there. It's a
real place! And I believe I can build that world, just as
I see it.

I must take this leap.

AZUCAR: It seems a taste for blood has whet everyone's appetite in this house.
So. We shall let Hunger decide.
If Mistress Ruby dares eat the cake— If I see that the cake has been eaten, then I will open the door for you to make your leap.

ZURI: The angels are with me, Azucar.

AZUCAR: And so it is.

(Blackout)

Scene 8:
Bedroom. Morning.

(ZURI packs EMILY's things.)

(EMILY flutters about the room, clearly desperate for ZURI's forgiveness. ZURI keeps her back turned while focused on her task.)

EMILY: I shall travel the world as a missionary one day.
(Beat)
Much better than being a wife locked away in a house with crying babies. Wouldn't you agree?
—I am frightened of her, Zuri!

(Silence)

(ZURI turns to face EMILY)

EMILY: Sorry.
(Beat)
I'm so very sorry.

ZURI: You almost had me killed last night.

EMILY: Father would never harm you.

ZURI: I've never been safe with you.

EMILY: Our sisterhood is true, Zuri.

ZURI: Sisterhood means you'd refuse to serve what the men kill for feast. We can never be sisters as long as I am on the plate.

EMILY: I want to repair our bond. No one means more to me than you. Truth!

(ZURI *puts her hands on* EMILY's *shoulders and slowly pushes her down onto her knees.* ZURI *then begins to circle* EMILY.)

ZURI: I think your Aunt Ruby wants to take me from this house. I think. she intends. to kill me.

(EMILY *puts her hands over her ears and hides.*)

ZURI: No! No. Sisters listen.

EMILY: Yes, yes, of course.

ZURI: Now. You. will tell me. a secret.
You will tell me. your secrets.

EMILY: …I was so frightened last night. I'd never slept in my bed without you.
So I played with the Eye. Until dawn.
I didn't realize until it was too late that I'd pressed it inside of myself, swallowed it with my tiny mouth, like a chicken taking back its egg.

ZURI: And where is it now?

EMILY: Inside of me.
I've been holding myself tight.
I thought if I held the Eye inside it would see how much I love you and didn't mean to cause you harm.

ZURI: Can the Eye speak?

EMILY: Yes!

ZURI: Did the eye speak to you?

EMILY: …Yes.

ZURI: And what did the eye say?

EMILY: …That it wants a body.

ZURI: Whose body?

EMILY: The buried bodies.

ZURI: Why?

EMILY: The eye wants to see everything kept hidden.
To glimpse the present and know itself.

ZURI: What is the present?

EMILY: The present is a Light. Sight is the gift.

ZURI: Stand up.
Close your eyes.
Reach inside and remove the egg.

(EMILY follows instructions. When she produces the egg in her hand, the egg is now red.)

EMILY: Does this mean we're sisters now?

ZURI: Do you wish us to be like our mothers?

EMILY: No.
(Beat)
I don't want to be dead.

ZURI: Then I am the gardener now.

EMILY: Yes.

ZURI: And I intend to plant a new garden.

EMILY: A Paradise?

ZURI: Outside of time.

EMILY: I want to live there with you!

ZURI: You'll have to shed your skin.

EMILY: I'll shed my kin.

ZURI: Your skin.

EMILY: I'll shed my skin, my kin, and my sin!

ZURI: Are you prepared to see what's been buried?

EMILY: Yes. The Eye chose me.

ZURI: Tell me then…what do the dead ever want?

EMILY: A witness!

ZURI: Good.
Then here is a body: We are true cousins. By blood. We share the same grandfather. Thus Ruby is my aunt too. Another body: Your father likes to play his own games with me at night. Last night he wanted to—
(She whispers the rest into EMILY's ear.)

(AZUCAR enters and looks them both over.

AZUCAR: Are you prepared to serve?

(EMILY and ZURI mirror each other; both hold an eerie pose and nod, yes.)

Scene 9:
Dining room. Morning.

(EMILY and PHILIP are seated at the table. He has a horrible headache and it shows. Something is tied tight around his head as a form of headache relief.)

(ZURI stands in the corner fanning the table.)

(AZUCAR enters carrying hard boiled eggs and blackberry jam.)

PHILIP: Where is Mistress Ruby?

AZUCAR: In the kitchen. She's banished me. Said she can't trust my hands to make her tea.

PHILIP: From which bottle did you pour my drink last night, Azucar?

(ZURI and AZUCAR exchange a glance: EMILY notices.)

AZUCAR: Ahh. The last little swallow from the bottle in the kitchen. The one I use for baking. Dark rum for a dark night.

PHILIP: Good thing it was the last of it. Far too strong an effect for my liking. I do not expect to wake up with a headache by this name again.

AZUCAR: No, never again, Master Philip.

ZURI: Master Philip? I made you a special drink. Sometimes small sips of the pain can soothe a sick stomach, no?

(ZURI *offers* PHILIP *the drink. He takes it.*)

PHILIP: My sweet clever girl.

ZURI: Here, let me tighten your knot a bit to squeeze that headache out.

(ZURI *tightens* PHILIP'*s knot.*)

EMILY: Will you be serving the leftover cake, Azucar?

PHILIP: *(Slurpy)* Yes, cake would be a treat.

AZUCAR: I'm afraid I'll have to throw it to the dogs. Zuri spilled a bottle of liquid charcoal onto it. Now I have to make another.

EMILY: Two cakes!

AZUCAR: Another bottle of liquid charcoal. The cake is only baked once a year. You know that, muñeca.

EMILY: Yes. I see.

PHILIP: Check on Ruby for us, Azucar.

AZUCAR: She would have my head.

EMILY: Shall we begin without her?

PHILIP: She'll want to say a prayer before we begin.

EMILY: And what do you want, Father? What do you truly, truly, truly want?

PHILIP: Enough of your babbling, Emily.

EMILY: Wash It-Cut It/ Smell It-Eat It.

PHILIP: I'm in no mood for one of your games, not on this/ particular morning.

EMILY: Are you there, Aunt Ruby?

PHILIP: Besides as the Lord of this manor / I explain myself to no one!

EMILY: Will you be joining us at the table, Aunt Ruby?

(RUBY *enters with tea in hand. Her lips, teeth and tongue are blackened by the charcoal in the cake.*)

(+AZUCAR+)

(+ZURI+)

(+EMILY+)

RUBY: We discussed yelling through the house, Emily. That will never stand at the convent. My chair, Azucar.

(AZUCAR *ignores* RUBY's *command.*)

RUBY: Philip you look like you've been dug out of a grave.

PHILIP: *(Tickled)* And you dear Ruby, you look like… salvation.

RUBY: Been swilling more than tea this morning? Your usual breakfast? Never mind. It matters not. I'll gladly step in to bless this table with a proper grace.
Bow your heads.
(She bows her head.)

(EMILY *studies* RUBY. PHILIP *studies* ZURI.)

(AZUCAR *lifts her shawl over her head and covers her face orisha-style.*)

RUBY: Dear Heavenly Father: Keep watch over our souls in this savage land. Deliver us from the darkness always stationed at the door. We accept our burdens with your holy grace. May the Light of the Lord bless our meal, our hearts, and this day. Amen.

(PHILIP's head drops back against his chair, eyes and mouth agape.)

RUBY: Emily, pass me the blackberry jam, dear.

(A subtle lighting change should indicate the psychological space being occupied.)

(AZUCAR shifts her pose, but remains veiled.)

(ZURI steps toward RUBY with a silver platter that gleams like a sword. She lowers the platter so that it obscures RUBY's face from the audience.)

(EMILY moves to sniff PHILIP, then repositions to daintily hold her egg just above his open throat.)

(ZURI flips the platter forward. The platter's final position should be set so that it rests against RUBY's throat.)

(ZURI continues to hold the platter with one hand, as the other hand reaches into her hair/bun and pulls out a knife like a pin.)

(EMILY and ZURI perform repetitive murderous motions [almost stabbing RUBY's throat then pulling back/ almost dropping the egg into PHILIP's throat then pulling back] in a stylized beat, as if they were haunted figurines in a cuckoo clock. The tone is ethereal madness.)

(We hear the sound of a violent ocean.)

(Fadeout)

END OF PLAY

www.ingramcontent.com/pod-product-compliance
Lightning Source LLC
Chambersburg PA
CBHW052219090426
42741CB00010B/2597